A Guide for Using

The Magic School Bus®
and
the Electric Field Trip

in the Classroom

Based on the book written by Joanna Cole

This guide written by Ruth M. Young, M.S. Ed.

©1999 Scholastic Inc. Based on *The Magic School Bus*® book series
©Joanna Cole and Bruce Degen. All rights reserved.
Experiments ©1999 Teacher Created Materials, Inc.

Teacher Created Materials, Inc.
6421 Industry Way
Westminster, CA 92683
www.teachercreated.com.
©*2000 Teacher Created Materials, Inc.*
Reprinted, 2004
Made in U.S.A.
ISBN-1-57690-082-7

Edited by
Walter Kelly, M.A.

Illustrated by
Howard Chaney

Table of Contents

Introduction

The use of literature can enhance the study of science. The key to selecting these books is to check them for scientific accuracy and appropriateness for the level of the students. The Magic School Bus® series, written by Joanna Cole, is an outstanding example of books which can help students enjoy and learn about science. These books are delightfully written and scientifically accurate, thanks to the thorough research done by the author as she writes each of her books.

This Science/Literature unit is directly related to *The Magic School Bus® and the Electric Field Trip*. It is designed to help you present exciting lessons for your students so that they can develop their understanding and appreciation of electricity–its nature and functions. The activities in this unit are particularly appropriate for intermediate and middle grades. Teachers who use this unit will find two lessons to do before they read the book with their students. These introductory lessons may serve as a means of assessing the present knowledge levels of the students.

The class should then read the book and follow up with a variety of hands-on science lessons. These lessons are spin-offs from reports written by Ms. Frizzle's students or activities which extend the learning gleaned from the students' experiences on the electric field trip.

Before the Book

The Activities: These two activities will serve as pre-assessments of the students' knowledge about the source of the electricity which comes through a wall socket and about how we use electricity.

How Does the Power Reach the Plug?

Materials: work sheet (page 5), overhead projector, pencils, rulers, colored pens or crayons

Procedure

1. When students are not in the classroom, write "How does the power reach the plug?" on a transparency on the overhead projector. Do not plug the projector into the wall. After the students are assembled, turn on the projector. When it doesn't light, let the students offer explanations for the problem. Eventually, someone will discover that the plug is not connected to the socket. Put the plug into the socket so the light in the projector comes on.

2. Ask students why the projector had to be plugged into the socket before it worked. Let them discuss this until they bring out the idea that power is coming from the wall socket that can only get into the projector through the wire.

3. Distribute to each student a copy of the work sheet How Does the Power Reach the Plug? and read the instructions to them.

4. As the students work, monitor their progress to be sure they are putting in all their ideas.

5. Once the drawings are completed, let students color them.

Closure

- When the students have completed their drawings, let them share in small groups.

- Based on what they learn, students will make other drawings at the end of this unit and compare them with their original drawings. Collect the original drawings and save them.

How Do We Use Electricity?

Materials: lined chart paper, felt pens, parent letter (page 6)

Procedure

1. Divide the students into small groups and let them brainstorm the ways we use electricity. Tell them to list these on paper.

2. Hang the chart paper in front of the class and have each group tell what they have listed. Add new items which students may have thought of to add to this final list.

Home Assignment

- Distribute the parent letter for students to take home. Read it with them so they understand that they are to bring back a list of at least three items not already on the class list. Have them copy the class list onto the letter.

- Allow time in the next day to collect the students' lists and add to them to the class chart.

Name _____

Date _____

How Does the Power Reach the Plug?

Finish the drawing to show where you think the power comes from that runs into the wall socket so that the overhead projector lamp can be turned on. Be sure to label the parts of your drawing to explain what they are.

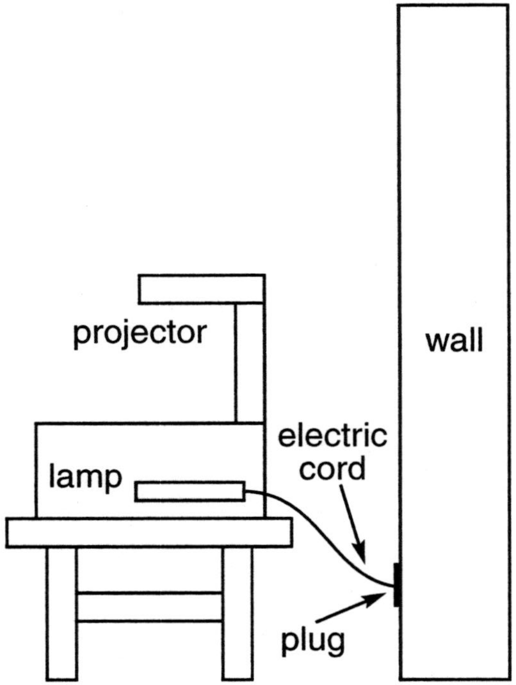

wall

electric cord

plug

projector

lamp

Parent Letter

Date _____

Dear Parents,

We are beginning a study of electricity and have made a list of the ways we use electricity. Our list is shown below.

_____   _____   _____

_____   _____   _____

_____   _____   _____

_____   _____   _____

Your child has been asked to look around the house and talk with you to find at least three other uses of electricity. Please help your child with this task, and then have him or her list the additional uses below.

_____   _____   _____

The student should bring the list back to school tomorrow so it can be added to the class chart.

Our study will last for a few weeks. Be sure to ask your child what he or she is learning about electricity during this time.

Sincerely,

About Author Joanna Cole

Joanna Cole was born on August 11, 1944, in New York. She attended the University of Massachusetts and Indiana University before receiving her B.A. from the City College of University of New York in 1967.

Joanna Cole loved science as a child. "I always enjoyed explaining things and writing reports for school. I had a teacher who was a little like Ms. Frizzle. She loved her subject. Every week she had a child do an experiment in front of the room and I wanted to be that child every week," she recalls. It's no surprise that when she was a child Cole's favorite book was *Bugs, Insects, and Such.*

Ms. Cole has worked as an elementary school teacher, a librarian, and a children's book editor. Combining her knowledge of children's literature with her love of science, she decided to write children's books. Her first book was *Cockroaches* (1971), which she wrote because there had never been a book written about the insect before. "I had ample time to study the creature in my low-budget New York apartment!"

Teachers and children have praised Ms. Cole's ability to make science interesting and understandable. Her *Magic School Bus*® series has now made science funny as well. Cole says that before she wrote this series, she had a goal to write good science books telling stories that would be so much fun to read that readers would read them even without the science component.

Readers across the country love the *Magic School Bus*® series and enjoy following the adventures of the wacky science teacher, Ms. Frizzle. Joanna Cole works closely with Bruce Degen, the illustrator for this series, to create fascinating and scientifically accurate books for children.

At times, even a successful writer finds it scary to begin writing a new book. That was the way Ms. Cole felt before beginning to write the *Magic School Bus*® series. She says, " I couldn't work at all. I cleaned out closets, answered letters, and went shopping—anything but sit down and write. But eventually I did it, even though I was scared."

Joanna Cole says kids often write their own *Magic School Bus*® adventures. She suggests they just pick a topic and a place for a field trip. Do a lot of research about the topic. Think of a story line and make it funny. Some kids even like to put their own teachers into their stories.

The Magic School Bus®
and
The Electric Field Trip

by Joanna Cole
(Scholastic, 1997)
(Canada, Scholastic; UK, Scholastic Ltd; AUS, Ashton Scholastic Party Ltd.)

Ms. Frizzle's students, studying electricity and its uses, prepare to go on a field trip to the power plant, but, knowing the Friz, this will not be an ordinary excursion. Accompanying the students is Ms. Frizzle's niece, Dottie, a miniature of her aunt in appearance and enthusiasm.

Ms. Frizzle tells Dottie and the students how moving electrons, jumping from atom to atom, create an electric current as they run through a wire from the wall plug into the motor of a fan. The students also learn how a magnet can make an electric current.

Suddenly, there is a flash of lightning and a clap of thunder. The electricity goes off, leaving the classroom dark. Ms. Frizzle orders everyone onto the bus. They soon find the problem along the road. Lightning has knocked a tree down onto the power line. Realizing the danger of this, the Friz spins the bus into a U-turn and drives off. The bus finally arrives at the power plant, where the children receive heat-proof suits to begin their tour. Ms. Frizzle pushes a button on the dashboard, and the bus becomes a coal dump-truck. Before they know it, they are being poured out of the bus, into the coal chute, and then into the furnace. The next stop is the boiler where water turns into steam, but they don't stay long. Soon they follow the steam into the turbine where the blades spin them around, propelling them onward. They pass with dizzying speed around the shaft which is turned by the turbine. Moving into the generator, they find the source of the electric current being created by a huge magnet moving inside the coils.

The current flows into power lines leading out of the plant at 24,000 volts. Ms. Frizzle, Dottie, and the students go with the flow, shrinking smaller to fit between the spaces in the wire where the electrons are jumping around. They follow the lines into town, dodging electrons as they go. They pass through transformers which decrease the voltage and then into a light bulb at the library. Along with electrons, they are squeezed through the filament, which gives off heat and light. They flow into a toaster at Joe's Diner to see the electric current heating the coils. Next, they visit Phoebe's house, where Grandma uses electricity in her power saw. Inside the motor, they find electromagnets moving a rotor that connects to the saw blade.

The Friz next takes them through an outlet into the wires in the walls and out another outlet into the vacuum cleaner wire. They get stuck in the vacuum cleaner when Grandpa switches it off to watch TV. Finally, Grandpa switches on the vacuum, and they follow the electric path back to school where they pop out of a hole in the insulation of the waxing machine wire.

The Radiometer

The Story: Ms. Frizzle's classroom always has appropriate science displays to add interest to lessons she presents her students. On the windowsill of her classroom sits a radiometer (page 11).

Demonstration: The objective is to launch the students' imaginations into determining what causes the vanes of the radiometer to move.

Materials: radiometer (see Resources, page 48,) overhead projector, three feet (91 cm) of electric wire, radiometer picture (page 10), transparency of How a Radiometer Works (page 11), table, box

Preparation

- Set up this demonstration without any students in the classroom. Place the box on top of a covered table. Tape one end of the electric wire to the center of the box and hide the other under the table. Place the radiometer on the box over the wire so it seems to be connected to the wire.

- Arrange the projector so its light will fall on the radiometer. Turn on the light to be sure it is close enough to spin the radiometer vanes. The students should be able to see the radiometer clearly, as well as the electric wire leading from it.

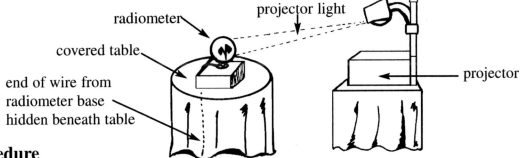

Procedure

1. Turn on the projector lamp so the vanes are spinning before the students come into the room.
2. Call their attention to the radiometer (do not mention the name of the instrument) and tell them to watch what is happening inside.
3. Ask them if they can explain what makes the vanes move.
4. Pull the wire out from under the table to show it is not plugged into the wall, although the vanes continue to spin.
5. Turn off the light so the students can see that the vanes slowly stop spinning. When they have stopped, turn on the light again. Ask the students what is needed to make the vanes spin.
6. Divide the students into small groups (or let them work alone). Distribute a picture of the radiometer and let them look closely at it. Tell them to draw what they see inside the globe and then show what they think makes it work.

Closure

- Let the students share their drawings. Use How a Radiometer Works for further explanation. Ask the students if it will work without air in it. (*No.*)

- Have the students try different light sources. (*The brighter the light, the faster the vanes will spin.*)

The Radiometer *(cont.)*

To the Teacher: Make copies of these radiometer pictures and cut them out to distribute to students.

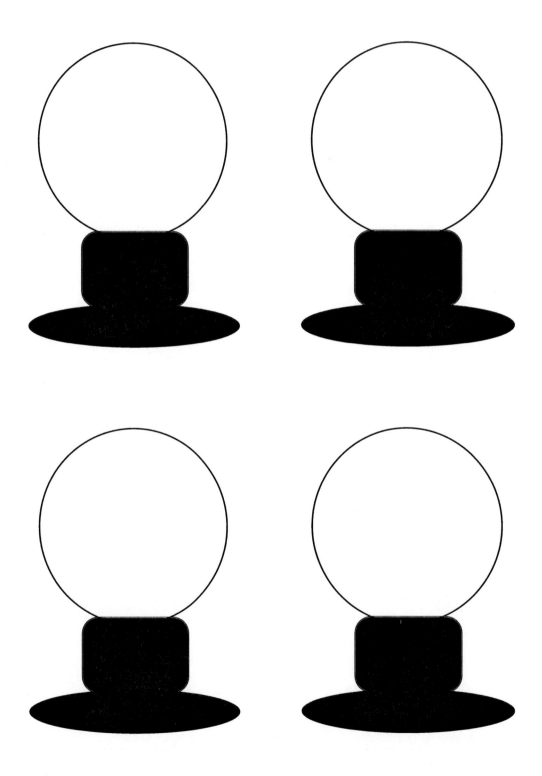

How a Radiometer Works

The *radiometer* was invented by William Crookes in the early 1900s. He wanted to prove that light is made of particles that press on a surface when they hit it. The radiometer is a glass bulb with most of the air pumped out before it is sealed. The air molecules can move around freely since there are fewer of them.

Small metal paddles called *vanes* are fastened to a glass cap that sits on top of a pin coming out of a glass stem at the bottom. This cap can spin around on top of the pin.

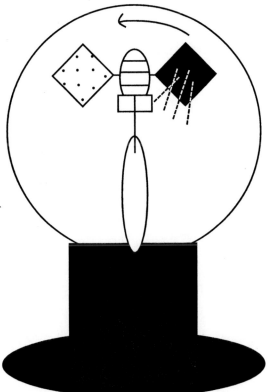

direction of spin

One side of the vane is a light color which does not absorb much heat. The air molecules near this side move slowly.

The other side of the vane is dark and absorbs more heat energy. It becomes warmer than the lighter side. Air molecules become warmer on this side and bounce off the surface. This pushes the vanes around, always spinning them in the same direction.

If there is no air inside the bulb, will the vanes spin?

What will happen if the light is brighter? dimmer?

Testing Magnets

The Story: Ms. Frizzle's class learns about magnetism. Wanda reports that magnets have two poles that push or pull when close together (page 32).

Activity: Students play with magnets to discover poles and how they interact.

Materials:

- circle, bar, horseshoe, and marble magnets (See Resources on page 48.)
- string, paper clips, and pencils which fit the circle magnet hole
- transparency and copies of Testing Magnets data sheet (page 13)
- parent letter (page 14)

Procedure

1. Divide students into small groups, providing each with an assortment of magnets, pieces of string, 20 paper clips, and a pencil. Allow students time to explore their magnets, holding them close together, suspending them from a string, and stacking them on the pencil. Challenge each group to create tricks to share with the class. Encourage them to try unusual things so not all will demonstrate the same tricks.

2. Have each group demonstrate its trick for the other students. Possibilities may include these:
- balancing one magnet on edge, suspended above another
- suspending circle magnets above each other on a pencil
- piling up marble magnets, suspending them in a string, or using them to chase other marble magnets across the table
- suspending a paper clip from a string and having it hang at an angle while being tugged by a magnet below it
- showing the strength of various magnets by using paper clips
- placing a magnet on the desktop and moving it around with another magnet below the desktop

3. Discuss what students learned from the magnets. Be sure they have discovered these facts:
- When magnets are close, they pull together (attract) or push apart (repel).
- When two magnets attract, turning one over (circle or horseshoe) or end-for-end (bar) will reverse the action.
- Magnets vary in strength.
- Magnetism passes through wood, paper, glass, and most other materials.
- Magnetism extends beyond the magnet and can attract or repel from a distance.

Closure (assessment)

Distribute the Testing Magnets data sheet to all and have them complete it. Using the transparency, discuss the results, noting that they may vary, depending on how students turned their magnets.

Home Assignment

Distribute the parent letter. Explain that students are to make lists and show shapes of magnets used in their homes.

Testing Magnets *(cont.)*

Name _____ Date _____

Show what happens when these two magnets come together.

| S | | S |

Explain how this feels.

_____

_____

Show what happens when these two magnets come together.

| N | | S |

Explain how this feels.

_____

_____

Stack three circle magnets on the pencil. Using the picture, show what happens to the magnets.

Explain what makes the magnets do this.

_____

_____

_____

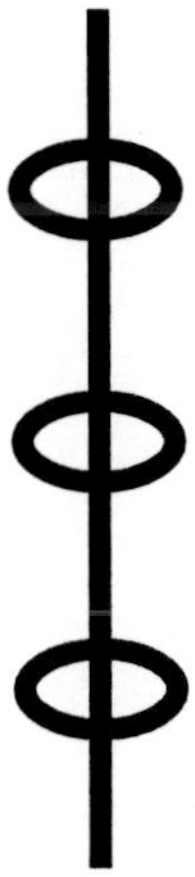

Change only one of the magnets on the pencil by turning it over. Make a drawing on the stick to show what happens.

Explain why the magnets change.

_____

_____

_____

Use two horseshoe magnets. Place them together as shown in the drawing. Show what happens when they are in this position.

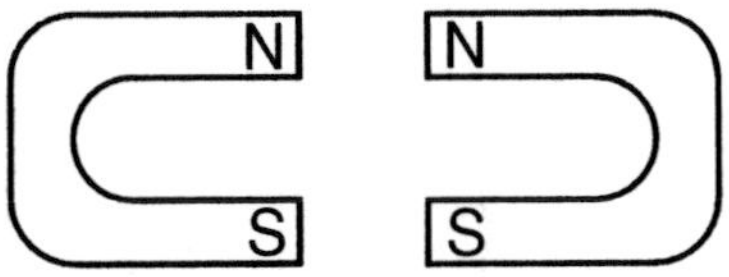

Explain what makes the magnets do this.

_____

_____

Turn one of the magnets over and place them together as shown in the drawing. Show what happens when you change the magnet's position.

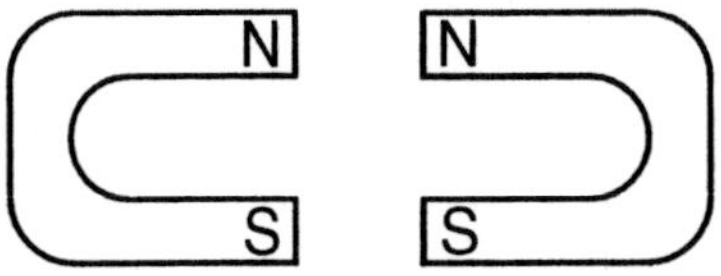

Explain what makes the magnets do this.

_____

_____

Parent Letter for Magnets

Date _____

Dear Parents:

Your child is learning about magnets and has been asked to find those which are used at home. Please help the student in his or her search. When a magnet is found, the student should write it on the list. If possible, he or she should draw the shape of the magnet.

Where This Magnet Is Used	Shape of the Magnet

Each student needs to bring this list to school tomorrow to share it during our science class. Our study of magnets will continue for several days. Ask your child to tell you what he or she is learning.

Thanks for your help.

Sincerely,

Seeing the Magnetic Field

Activity: Students make the magnetic field visible by using iron filings.

Materials

- bar and horseshoe magnets
- iron filings (See Resources on page 48.)
- glass pie plate
- aluminum pie pans

- small jars
- pieces of nylon stocking
- rubber bands
- overhead projector

Preparation

Pour some iron filings into the jars and place a piece of nylon stocking over each of them. Hold this in place with the rubber band.

Demonstration

1. Review the concepts students learned about magnetism in the previous activity.

2. On the overhead projector, place two bar magnets so they repel each other. Ask students if they can see anything which is pushing them apart. (*no*)

3. Rotate one of the magnets and demonstrate the attracting action. Again, ask if students can see anything which pulls them together (*no*).

4. Explain that this invisible force is called the *magnetic field,* which exists around all magnets. Tell them that, using tiny pieces of iron called *iron filings,* you will show them where this field is.

5. Place one bar magnet on the projector and put the glass pie plate over it. Sprinkle the filings into the plate, over the magnet below it. Cover the plate with a fine mist of iron at both ends and around the magnet. The iron will outline the magnetic field.

6. Ask the students to look at the pattern which is formed by the filings and tell where the magnet is strongest and how they know. (*The ends attract more iron and are therefore the strongest points.*)

7. Point out the arc of filings which join the two poles. Ask students to explain what is happening here. (*Opposite poles attract, and the iron filings outline this magnetic field arc.*)

8. Dump the filings onto a paper and then place another bar magnet on the stage. Turn the magnets so they attract. Separate the magnets so that they will not come together.

9. Place the pie plate on the magnets. Sprinkle the filings over the space between them. Have the students notice that the iron builds a bridge between the magnets, outlining the magnetic field that pulls them together.

Seeing the Magnetic Field *(cont.)*

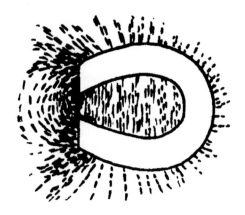

10. Dump the filings onto the paper and then turn one of the magnets around. Place the pie plate over the magnets. Tell the students to draw what they think the filings will look like this time. Sprinkle the filings between the magnets and show that they are pushed away by the poles. They leave an empty space between the poles of the magnets.

11. Show the magnetic field of a horseshoe magnet.

12. Point out the arc which joins the ends and ask why this occurs. (The magnetic field between the opposite poles at each end of the magnet is attracting. The iron filings outline this magnetic field.)

Closure

- Divide the students into small groups and provide each group with magnets, a jar of iron filings, two aluminum pie pans, and a piece of scrap paper.

- Explain that as the students use the iron filings to outline the magnet field, they must be sure the magnets do not touch the filings. If this happens, all filings will need to be removed by pulling them away from the magnet, which is very tedious and time consuming.

- Demonstrate how they should place the magnet(s) in one pie pan and then place the second pan over the magnet(s). They should sprinkle the filings into the top pie pan to see the pattern which occurs.

- They should dump the filings onto the scrap paper, keeping it well away from the magnets.

- Let the students experiment with a variety of magnets to see what patterns appear. They may place a piece of paper on the bottom of the pie pan to see the pattern better.

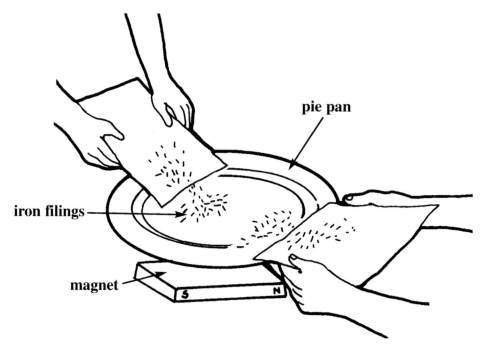

pie pan

iron filings

magnet

Magnetic Pictures

Activity: Students make pictures of the magnetic field.

Materials

- same materials used in previous lesson
- sunprint paper (See Resources on page 48.)
- basin of water and pieces of newspaper

Preparation

Make examples of magnetic field prints as follows:

- Place a magnet in an aluminum pie pan and put another pie pan over the magnet.
- Put a sheet of sunprint paper (blue side up) in the top pie pan over the area where the magnet is located below.
- Sprinkle iron filings over the surface of the paper so that they show the magnetic field.
- Carefully carry both pie pans out into sunlight. Put them in full sunlight for a few minutes. Watch the paper fade to white.
- Take the pans into the classroom, dump off the iron filings, and place the paper in the basin of water until it turns back to blue. White areas will remain where iron filings outlined the magnetic field.
- Spread newspaper on a table. Remove the sunprint paper from the water, place it facedown on the newspaper, and cover it with more newspaper and a heavy book to keep it flat. Remove the paper after 10 minutes. The sunprint can now be placed faceup to dry.
- Make two more pictures, using other magnets to show the repelling and then the attracting fields.

Procedure

1. Set up the glass pie pan and a magnet on the stage of the overhead projector. Demonstrate how to outline the magnetic field with the iron filings.
2. Explain that you will show how to make a picture of the magnetic field. Show the examples you prepared before class.
3. Demonstrate how this is done, using the pie plate over the magnet on the overhead projector. Use a square of paper (not sunprint) to illustrate how to place the paper. Explain how students will use two pie pans and carry them out to sunlight.
4. Group the students and distribute all materials except sunprint paper. Explain that this paper is sensitive to light and must be kept blue side down until ready for use.
5. Distribute one paper to each group and have a member of each group place his or her name on the back (white side). Let these students make a sunprint picture. When they return to class with their prints, dump off the filings and give them a new sunprint paper for the next group member.

Closure (assessment)

- Pin the sunprint pictures to a bulletin board. Put a number below each picture. Let the students list the numbers in columns labeled "Repelling" (pushing), "Attracting" (pulling), and "Both."
- Discuss the answers with the students.

Making a Magnet

Activity: Students will turn a steel pin into a magnet.

Materials: steel straight pins, circle magnets, iron filings

Procedure

1. Summarize what students have learned thus far about the properties of magnets. Be sure they mention that a magnet has a field around it that attracts or repels another magnet.

2. Tell them that they are going to make a magnet out of something which is not already a magnet. Explain that in order to do this, the object to be magnetized must be made of a metal that will attract to a magnet. Show them the straight pins and let them know they are going to magnetize them.

3. Divide the students into small groups. Give each group about a teaspoon of iron filings on a piece of paper. Give each student a magnet and pin. Caution them not to get their magnets near the iron filings.

4. Have the students dip the points of their pins into the iron filings. The pins may attract some filings. If so, have them clean off the filings.

5. Show the students how to lay a pin on the table and hold it down firmly with a finger by pressing down on the head. They should then stroke the pin with the circle magnet. The magnet should be pressed hard against the pin for each stroke and stroked about 50 times in one direction only.

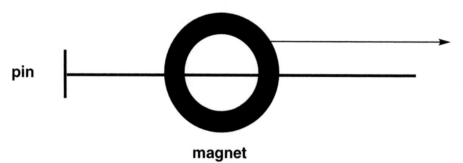

6. Let the students test the strength of their new pin magnets by again dipping them into the filings. If a pin has been magnetized, it should pick up more of the filings. If this does not happen, students should repeat the magnetizing procedure.

7. Have each student work with a partner and test the pins for positive and negative reactions. This is done by laying one pin on the table and bringing the other pin tip to tip with it. If the ends are the same, they will repel, if different, they will attract. Let them try turning one of the pins to see if the reaction changes, just as it does with real magnets.

Closure

Make a transparency of Making a Magnet (page 19) to explain how this was done.

Making a Magnet *(cont.)*

In an ordinary pin, the atoms are not arranged in any particular order. As you run the magnet over the pin, the atoms line up with the positive end pointing one way and the negative the other. Stroking the pin many times strengthens this alignment.

The pin is only a temporary magnet, however, and the magnetism gets weaker with time. If the pin is hit hard with a hammer or is heated, it will lose its magnetism.

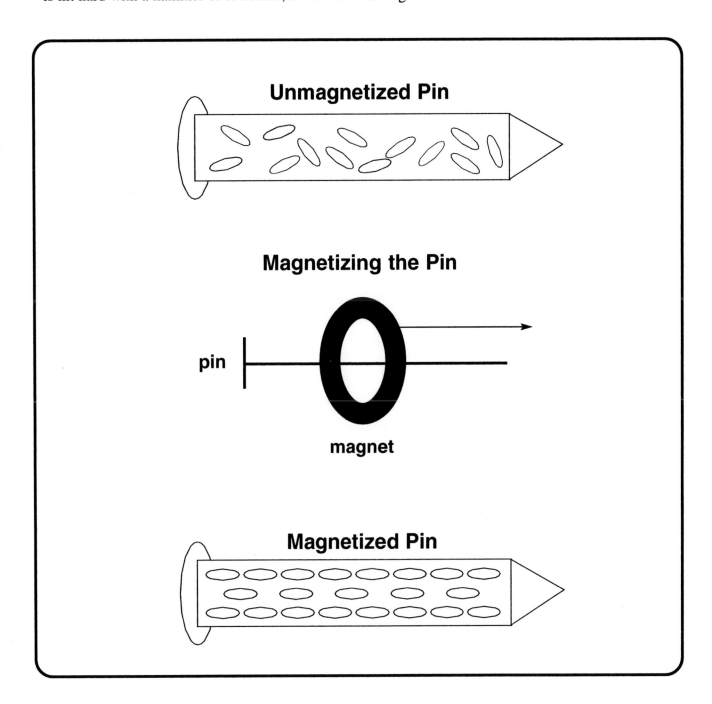

Unmagnetized Pin

Magnetizing the Pin

pin

magnet

Magnetized Pin

The Electron Dance

The Story: Ms. Frizzle tells the students about the atom (pages 8 and 9) as an introduction to electricity.

Activity: Students will do a dance to simulate the action of electrons within an atom.

Materials

- two basketballs labeled "neutron" (+/-)
- two volleyballs labeled "proton" (+)
- two Ping-Pong balls labeled "electron" (-)
- transparency of Parts of an Atom (page 22)
- four file cards to be used as labels on large balls
- two 8 ½" x 11" (21 cm x 28 cm) pieces of tagboard labeled "Nucleus" and "The Atom"
- nine feet (2.7 m) of string with chalk tied on one end and a loop on the other

Preparation

Select a helper to make the outlines on a large paved area (e.g., playground blacktop) for the electron dance. Use the chalk on the end of the string to draw one circle on the blacktop area to represent the location of the nucleus. The helper should stand in the middle and hold the loop end of the string while the end with the chalk is stretched to draw a circle of a two-foot (61 cm) radius. Draw two larger circles with their centers in the middle of the nucleus circle. The circles should have radii of six and nine feet respectively (1.8 m and 2.7 m). These are the orbits of the electrons.

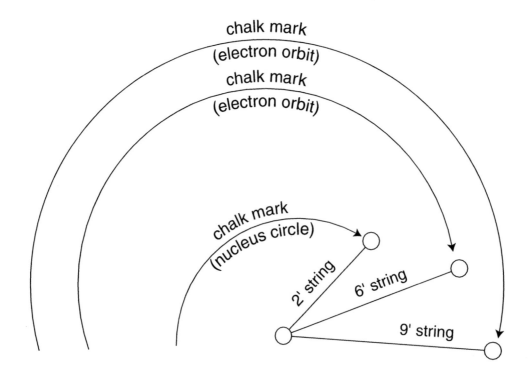

The Electron Dance *(cont.)*

Procedure

1. Review pages 8 and 9 of the story where Ms. Frizzle explains the atom to her class. Point out that the drawing shows the atom as a sphere.

2. Use the transparency of Parts of an Atom (page 22) to explain how an atom works. Explain how the students are to move outside to simulate an atom, including the motion of the electrons around the nucleus. Go to the area to be used for the simulation.

3. Select two students to be the electrons; give each of them a Ping-Pong ball.

4. Select two students to be neutrons; give them each a basketball marked "neutron."

5. Select two students to be protons; give them each a volleyball marked "proton."

6. Select two students to hold the large signs "Nucleus" and "The Atom."

7. Station the protons and neutrons inside the center circle. Place the student holding the "Nucleus" sign outside this circle.

8. Place the two electrons on the orbits.

9. Place the person with "The Atom" sign outside the outermost circle.

10. Remind students that the nucleus is made up of protons and neutrons, represented by larger balls since nearly all the mass of the atom is in its nucleus. Point out that the electrons have much less mass than the protons and neutrons.

11. Tell the "players" that on your signal, the electrons should begin running around the nucleus, staying on their circles. They do not need to orbit in the same direction. Stop the students after they have raced around the nucleus several times. Review the fact that although they were moving fast, and on the plane (the pavement), real electrons travel so fast and all around the nucleus that they would appear as a sphere, much like a bubble.

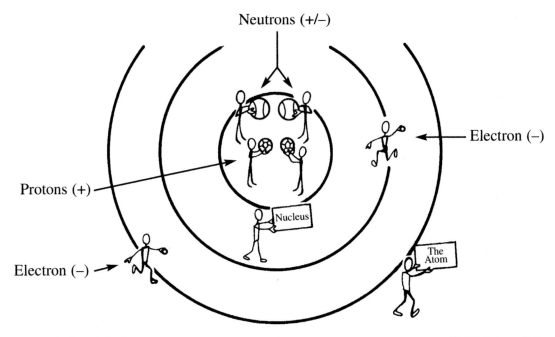

Parts of an Atom

Matter has mass and takes up space. Atoms are basic building blocks of matter. Atoms are made up of three types of particles: *protons, neutrons,* and *electrons*. Protons and neutrons make up most of the mass of the atom. In a 150-pound person, for example, 149 pounds and 15 ounces are protons and neutrons while only one ounce is electrons. The mass of an electron is very small.

The nucleus of the atom has both the protons and neutrons. Protons have a positive (+) charge, and neutrons have no (+/−) charge—they are neutral. Electrons orbit around the nucleus. They have a negative (−) charge. The electron orbits are spherical around the nucleus, not a flat plane like the orbits of the planets around the sun. The electrons move so fast that they form a shell around the nucleus, much like the blades of a fan, which prevents anything passing through them as they spin.

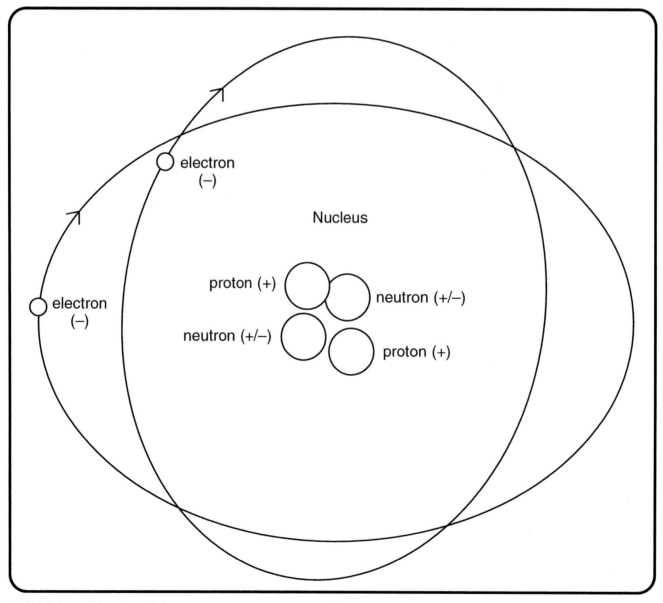

Static Magic

Activity: Students will experiment with static electricity.

Materials

- large balloons
- string
- chairs
- transparency of Static Cling (page 24)

Procedure

1. Ask the students if they have ever walked across a carpet, touched a lamp or doorknob, and felt a spark of electricity. Explain that this is static electricity. Tell them that they are going to use balloons to find out about static electricity.

2. Give each student a balloon and a six-inch (15 cm) piece of string. Let them work with a partner to inflate their balloons and tie the string around the top tightly to seal the air inside.

3. Have each pair of students place their chairs back to back, tie a three-foot (91 cm) string between the chairs, and then suspend their balloons from this string.

4. Let the students test what happens when they push the balloons together and then let them go. *(They should continue to hang separately.)*

5. Next instruct one of the partners in each group to rub a balloon vigorously against his or her hair and then let it hang. (These balloons should attract the other balloons.)

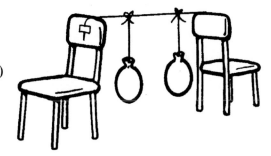

6. Have both partners in each group rub their balloons against their hair to see what happens. *(The balloons should now repel each other.)*

Closure

- Show the students the transparency Static Cling and use it to explain the balloon reactions.

- Ask the students how this attraction-repulsion reminds them of the magnetic field they learned about earlier. *(The electric field is like the magnetic field around a magnet.)*

- Explain that the north pole of a magnet is positive and the south pole is negative.

- Permit the students to play with static electricity, using their balloons. They can charge up the balloons with their hair and then hold them near the following objects:

  – hair on their arms.

  – string on the table.

  – small circles of paper from a hole-punch machine.

Static Cling

Normally, an atom has an equal number of electrons and protons, and so it is electrically neutral. If an atom gains some electrons, it becomes negatively charged. If an atom loses some electrons, it becomes positively charged. Atoms that have an electric charge—either positive or negative— are called *ions*.

Every particle is surrounded by an *electric field*. Charged particles exert a force on one another, even when not touching, because each electric field extends into the space around each particle.

Uncharged Particles

If two balloons are uncharged, they do not exert any force between them.

Particles with Unlike Charges

If one balloon is charged positively and the other negatively, their electric fields interact and pull them together.

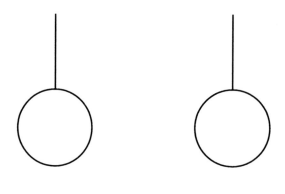

Particles with Like Charges

If two balloons are each negatively (or each positively) charged, their electric fields interact and cause them to move apart.

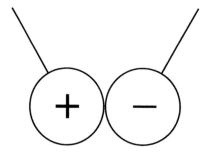

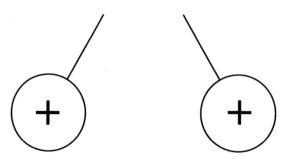

Using Electricity

The Story: Ms. Frizzle's students are already beginning their activities with electricity as they investigate connecting batteries to a light bulb and a bell (page 6).

Activity: Students investigate electricity, using batteries as a safe source of electrical current.

Materials

Each student will need a D battery and 2.5 volt light bulb (#41).

The entire class will need 100 feet (30 m) of #22 insulated copper wire and a wire cutter/stripper. (See Delta Educational in the Resources section, page 48, for bulbs and wire.)

Preparation

- Cut the wire into 10-inch (25 cm) lengths, making enough for one per student. Strip off about 1/2 inch (1 cm) of the insulation at each end of the wire.
- Check the batteries and bulbs to be sure they work. Connect them as shown below.

Procedure

1. Distribute one light bulb, wire, and battery to each student. Tell them to connect these to get the bulb to light. Permit the students enough time to experiment and to work past their first failures until many of the students have discovered how to do this.

2. Have one of the students who has successfully connected the light bulb go to the board and make a large drawing of how to connect the parts to make the bulb light. Let all the students try this method.

3. Encourage them to set to work again to discover at least four ways the wire can be connected to the bulb and battery in order to get the bulb to light.

Closure

- Have students make three more drawings on the board to show the other methods they have discovered to light the bulb.
- Distribute a paper to the students and have them draw the four methods. Check that they have shown exactly where the wire must touch the bulb and battery in order to light the bulb.

The Light Bulb

The Story: Dorothy Ann makes a report showing how the light bulb is made. The class passes through the light bulb filament at the library (pages 28 and 29).

Activity: Students investigate how a light bulb works.

Materials

- Each student will need batteries, bulbs, wire, magnifier, two 3" x 5" (8 cm x 13 cm) file cards, six inches (15 cm) string, crayon, and four pieces of clear tape

- Additional materials for the entire class are three or four 2.5–volt bulbs (burned out ones will do) and a variety of clear light bulbs.

- transparency of The Light Bulb (page 27)

Preparation

Carefully use wire strippers and other tools to remove the metal casing from the 2.5 volt bulbs. Wear gloves so you can hold the bulb as you work. Try to expose wires leading from the glass bulb into the base but preserve the connections between the wires and the base.

Procedure

1. Review the activity of lighting a bulb by using one wire and battery. When all students have a bulb lit, have them look at the glowing part (filament) with a magnifier, noting the filament shape (coiled) and how it is supported in the bulb.

2. Distribute file cards and tell students they are to fill each card with a large outline drawing of the bulb and its base. Next, they should draw all the details of what they see inside the bulb, as well as what is attached to the side and bottom of the metal casing. As they work, send the "dissected" bulbs around the room for students to examine, especially the wires and where these are connected.

Closure

- Have the students reconnect their light bulbs, using the four methods discovered in the previous lesson. Ask them to explain why it is important to make contact with the wire, the bulb, and the battery in a particular manner.

- Show the transparency (page 27) and discuss the features of the light bulb. Let students look at the other clear light bulbs to compare them with the small bulbs.

- Distribute the other file cards, crayon, string, and tape. Have the students draw a large battery on the file card. Using the string to represent the wire, they should tape the parts together to show how to light the bulb. Students should use the crayon to trace the flow of electricity from the battery through the light bulb filament and back to the battery (page 27). Also, notice Completing the Circuit, the three steps boxed in the transparency on page 27. You may wish to review these with the students more than once.

The Light Bulb *(cont.)*

100–watt bulb

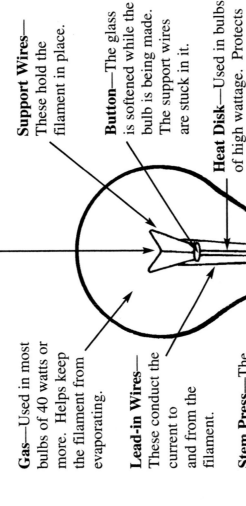

Support Wires—These hold the filament in place.

Button—The glass is softened while the bulb is being made. The support wires are stuck in it.

Heat Disk—Used in bulbs of high wattage. Protects the bottom of the bulb from heat.

Fuse—This helps keep the bulb from cracking and prevents blowing of electric fuses.

Base

Filament—The wire that heats up to *incandescence* (in-can-des-cents), or glowing, white heat. Edison used a cotton sewing thread burned to an ash as his first filament. Today, the filament is made of *tungsten*, which does not melt except under extreme heat.

Gas—Used in most bulbs of 40 watts or more. Helps keep the filament from evaporating.

Lead-in Wires—These conduct the current to and from the filament.

Stem Press—The glass and lead-in wires have an airtight seal here.

Exhaust Tube—Through this tube, air is taken out of the bulb and the gas is pumped in. The tube is sealed off so the base will fit over it.

2.5–volt bulb

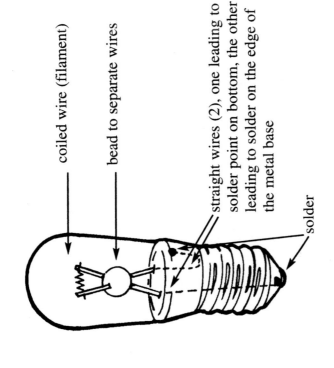

coiled wire (filament)

bead to separate wires

straight wires (2), one leading to solder point on bottom, the other leading to solder on the edge of the metal base

solder

Completing the Circuit

1. Current passes from the negative end of the battery through wire soldered to the side of the metal casing on the light bulb.

2. Current continues through this wire to the support wire attached to one side of the filament, across the filament, and back into the other support wire which is attached to the bottom of the bulb.

3. Current passes back into the positive end of the battery and then to the negative end where it flows into the wire again.

Making a Flashlight

The Story: The electrical workers have to shut off the power before they can safely repair the downed power line. They open breakers, which are like giant switches (page 16). The students discover more information about electric switches as they travel through the line and when they hear a report from Alex (page 38).

Activity: Students construct a simple flashlight with a switch.

Materials

- D–cell batteries
- cardboard tubes (e.g., toilet paper rolls)
- masking tapes

Preparation

Construct an example of a flashlight, using a bulb, two batteries, and one long wire. Use the cardboard tube to hold the batteries. Use the tape to hold the bulb on top of one battery and to make contact with the wire. Run the wire through the tube toward the bottom of the batteries. Use foil to make a switch at the bottom of the flashlight. When the switch makes contact between the wire and the bottom of the batteries, the bulb will light. The drawing below will help you to make this model.

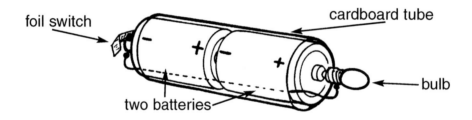

foil switch   cardboard tube

two batteries   bulb

Procedure

1. Group the students into pairs and give each pair two batteries, one wire, and one bulb. Let them work together to get the bulb to light. They will discover that the positive (+) end of one battery must make contact with the negative (-) end of the other battery in order for the bulb to light.

2. Give students the challenge of constructing a flashlight, using the materials they have plus a cardboard tube, a piece of foil, and masking tape. Tell them their flashlight must have a switch so that it can be turned on and off. Explain that when they are finished, each model will be demonstrated.

Closure

- Have students demonstrate how they made their flashlights. Darken the room and let each pair show how far their light will travel.

- Discuss the variations in flashlights and how improvements can be made.

Creating Electric Circuits

The Story: Arnold writes on "Do Electrons Run Only One Way in the Power Line?" (page 27)

Activity: Students construct simple circuits with batteries.

Materials (per student)

- two wires
- one battery
- one battery holder
  (See Related Materials on page 48 to locate a source for the of equipment.)
- How Do Circuits Work? data sheet (page 30)

- one light bulb
- one light bulb holder

Preparation

- Order bulb holders (sockets) and battery holders to be used for this lesson.
- Experiment with making circuits to be aware of problems students may encounter.

Procedure

1. Distribute the materials to each student and tell them they should assemble them to light the bulb.

2. Demonstrate how to use the connectors (Fahnestock clips) on the battery holder and sockets.

3. Ask the students to examine the contact points made on the light bulb. Have them explain how this is like the method they used when lighting their bulbs in the first lesson of this series. *(The bulb holder makes contact at the side and bottom of the bulb. Separate wires lead into each contact on the holder.)*

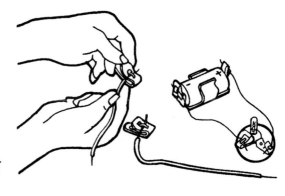

4. Distribute a file card to each student and have each make a drawing of his or her circuit, showing and labeling all the parts. When this is finished, have each student draw a line in pencil to show the flow of electricity from the battery to the bulb and back into the battery.

Closure

- Let students form pairs to try to combine their equipment to light up more than one bulb. They will discover that the placement of the batteries (+ connected to –) must be followed in order to light the bulbs.
- Make groups of three students and have them create more elaborate circuits.

Extender

Divide the students into groups and distribute the data sheet How Do Circuits Work? along with materials needed to complete these activites.

How Do Circuits Work?

Your group will need the following materials to do these activities:

- one battery
- six insulated wires
- one battery holder
- three light bulbs
- three light sockets

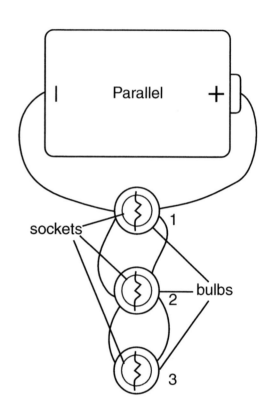

1. Unscrew the bulb in socket 1 just until it goes out. What happens to the bulbs in the other sockets?

   _____

2. Tighten the bulb again and then repeat this experiment by unscrewing one bulb at a time. Do the other bulbs go out?_____

3. Use a colored pencil and trace the electricity from the battery to bulbs 1, 2, and 3 and then back to the battery.

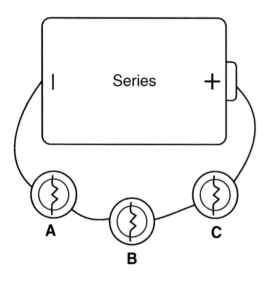

4. Unscrew the bulb in socket A. What happens to the other bulbs? _____

5. Repeat this by unscrewing one bulb at a time. What happens to the bulbs?_____

6. Use a colored pencil and trace the electricity from the battery to bulbs A, B, and C.

7. Compare the parallel and series circuits. Tell what is different about them when you unscrew the bulbs. _____

   _____

8. Explain why they are different._____

   _____

What Conducts Electricity?

The Story: Carlos writes a report about conductors and things which block the path of electricity (page 11).

Activity: Students will test a variety of items to see if they conduct electricity.

Materials: (per group)

- battery
- battery holder
- three wires
- socket
- light bulb

- variety of materials to check as conductors (including metal and nonmetal items such as coins, pipe cleaners, marble, foil, paper clips, cork, slices of lemon, cups of water, and sharpened pencils)

Procedure

1. Place the students into groups of 3 or 4 and distribute the materials needed to assemble their tester (see picture below). Have them hold the wires together to be sure the light works. When testing an item for conductivity, the wires should only touch the object, not each other. If the item is a conductor, the electricity will travel through it into wires.

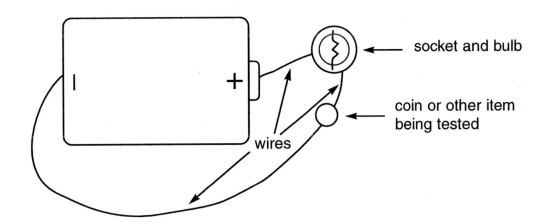

socket and bulb

coin or other item being tested

wires

2. Distribute a set of materials to each student. Have them sort the materials into three groups—those which they think will conduct electricity, those they think will not, and those which they are not sure will work. Collect this information from the groups by listing these items on the board.

3. Have the students test the items and re-sort their piles. Ask whether there were any surprises. (*The pencil lead will conduct electricity as well as the metal inside the pipe cleaner. Water and the lemon will conduct electricity if the wires are held close together. Water works even better when salt is added.*)

Constructing an Electromagnet

The Story: Tim writes a report on "How to Make an Electromagnet" (page 33). This requires some wire, a piece of iron or steel, and a battery.

Activity: Students will build an electromagnet and learn how it relates to building a simple electric motor.

Materials (per group)

- two batteries
- two battery holders
- long steel (iron) nail
- box of paper clips
- two feet (61 cm) insulated wire

- transparency of Making a Magnet (page 19)
- four inches (10 cm) insulated wire (Strip about one inch [2.5 cm] of insulation from the ends of each wire.)

Procedure

1. Review the properties of a magnet which students learned in earlier lessons. Discuss what types of material a magnet will pick up, as well as the strengths of different magnets.

2. Tell the students that they are going to see how to build a magnet from something that is not a magnet. Explain that they will use the electric current from a battery to do this.

3. Cluster the students into groups and distribute the materials to them, giving only one battery and battery holder to each group. Have them try to attract paper clips with the nail. (*It will not pick up any.*) Demonstrate how to assemble the battery, wire, and nail to create an electromagnet. The wire should be wound closely around the nail, leaving only about six inches (15 cm) at each end.

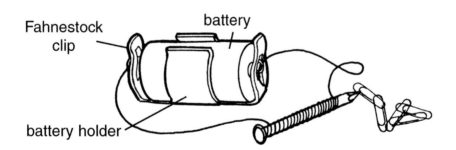

4. Let the students assemble their electromagnets and then see how many paper clips each will pick up. Discuss how the electricity flowing through the nail from the battery has made all the electrons line up in a north-south polar direction. Use the transparency Making a Magnet to compare this with the earlier lesson on magnetizing a pin with a magnet.

5. Have them experiment by adding a second battery. Let them devise ways to gather data to compare the differences in strength when using either one or two batteries.

6. Let them try picking up other items in the classroom with their electromagnets. (*They will find that electromagnets pick up the same things their magnets did.*)

Closure

Have the students design a switch to turn their electromagnets on and off. They may use paper clips, foil, or other metal pieces for the switch.

Building an Electric Motor

The Story: The students pass through the electric motor in the power saw being used by Phoebe's grandma. They discover that it uses electromagnets to make it work. (pages 34 and 35).

Demonstration: making a simple electric motor

Materials

- electric motor built according to instructions on page 34
- transparencies of Building a Simple Electric Motor and How the Motor Works (pages 34 and 35)
- transparency and copies of Putting the Motor to Work (page 36)

Preparation

Follow the instructions for building the electric motor. Experiment with the motor before presenting it to the class.

Helpful Hints: If the motor does not run properly, the suggestions below may help.

- Balance the coil on the end wires so that it hangs straight.
- Oil from hands may get on the wire ends; wipe them with a tissue.
- Lay the battery on its side on the table edge or at an angle.
- Be sure the loops on the paper clips are level with each other and making firm contact with the battery.
- The distance between the coil and magnet is important. Make sure the coil just barely misses the magnet as it rotates.

Procedure

1. Tell students you have built a simple motor. Show them the motor and use the transparency to explain how it was made. Demonstrate how it works. Turn the magnet over to show that this reverses the rotation of the coil.

2. Ask the students to suggest changes which may be made on the motor. These may include adding a second magnet on top of the first, adding another battery to see if the speed changes, or changing the coil to one with more wire, different wire, or different shape.

3. If the students are capable, cluster them in small groups and distribute the materials and instructions so they may create their own motors. Instructions may also be sent home for students to try building a motor with family help.

Closure

- Use the transparencies Building a Simple Electric Motor and How the Motor Works to show how the motor works.
- Show pages 34 and 35 of *The Magic School Bus® and the Electric Field Trip* for students to compare the diagram of how the saw motor works with that of the simple motor.
- Distribute a copy of Putting the Motor to Work to each student. Use the transparency to describe what they are to do. Display their finished drawings.
- Show the simple, humorous explanations for magnetism and electricity in *The Way Things Work* (see Resources, page 48).

Building an Electric Motor *(cont.)*

Materials

- needle-nosed and regular pliers
- small piece of fine-grain sandpaper
- D battery
- two regular–sized paper clips
- piece of packing tape

- one circular or rectangular ceramic magnet (Radio Shack carries these.)
- three feet (1 m) green enamel-coated magnet wire (available from Radio Shack, Catalog #278-1345A. The package includes three spools of magnetic wire; two are enamel–coated, and the third is uncoated copper wire. Use the green–coated wire.)

Preparation

- Cut the wire and wind it around a one-inch (2.5 cm) diameter object (e.g., large glue stick) to make a coil. Leave about three inches (8 cm) of wire uncoiled at each end. Wind each end wire around the coil on opposite sides. The last loop of wire should be placed under the previous one and tugged tightly to lock the coil of wire in place. Leave 2 inches (5 cm) extending from each side.

- Hold the coil vertically and lay the end wire on a flat surface. Use sandpaper to remove the enamel insulation from only one side of the end wire.

- Remove all the insulation from the other end wire.

- Bend the paper clips to act as supports for the end wires. Strengthen the paper clip with the pliers, leaving both ends curved. Twist the longer loop into a circle around a ballpoint pen.

- Attach the paper clips to each end of the battery with a strip of packing tape. These need to be positioned so they are straight and the loops are even with each other. The wire also needs to make a firm contact with the battery.

- Pass the end wires through the loops. Make them as straight as possible. Lay the battery on its side at the edge of the table or hold it upside down. Set the coil spinning by tapping it with your finger. If it doesn't spin properly, try spinning it the other way.

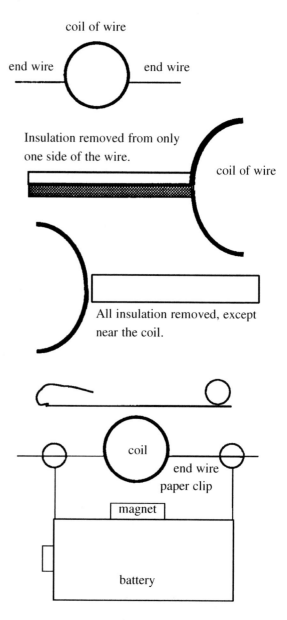

coil of wire

end wire   end wire

Insulation removed from only one side of the wire.

coil of wire

All insulation removed, except near the coil.

coil

end wire

paper clip

magnet

battery

How the Motor Works

Look at pages 34 and 35 of *The Magic School Bus® and the Electric Field Trip.* There is a great description of the way electromagnets create a motor which turns the power saw disk so Phoebe's grandma can cut the plank. The parts of a simple motor work in much the same way.

How the Motor Works

1. The battery is the power source, creating the electrical power chemically.

2. Current flows from the battery through the wire coil and creates an *electromagnet*.

3. One face of the coil becomes a north pole, the other a south pole.

4. The permanent magnet attracts its opposite pole on the coil and repels its like pole. One of the end wires is half-coated with insulation. The insulation stops the current for a split second. The coil continues to spin and rotates the like pole toward the magnet. It is repelled away, and the coil continues to spin.

5. The end wires, attached to the coil, also rotate and are the shaft of the motor.

6. The current flows back into the battery. As long as the battery continues to generate power, this flow of electrons continues and the coil rotates, turning the shaft.

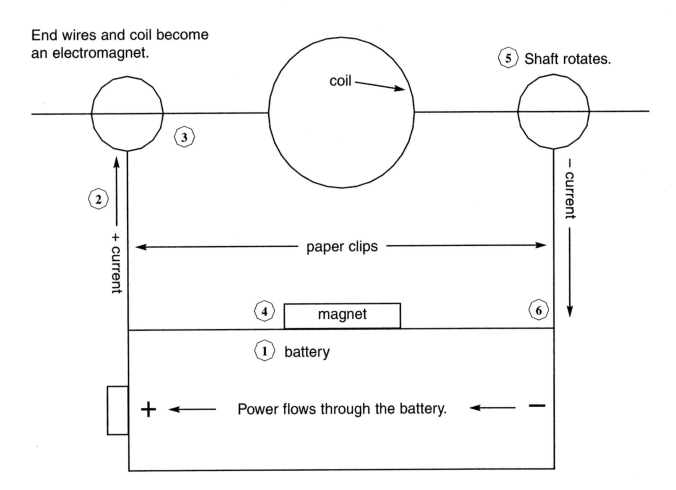

End wires and coil become an electromagnet.

coil

⑤ Shaft rotates.

③

② + current

− current

paper clips

④ magnet   ⑥

① battery

+ ← Power flows through the battery. ← −

Putting the Motor to Work

Add to this drawing to show an electric tool that could be operated by it. Be sure to label the parts of the drawing.

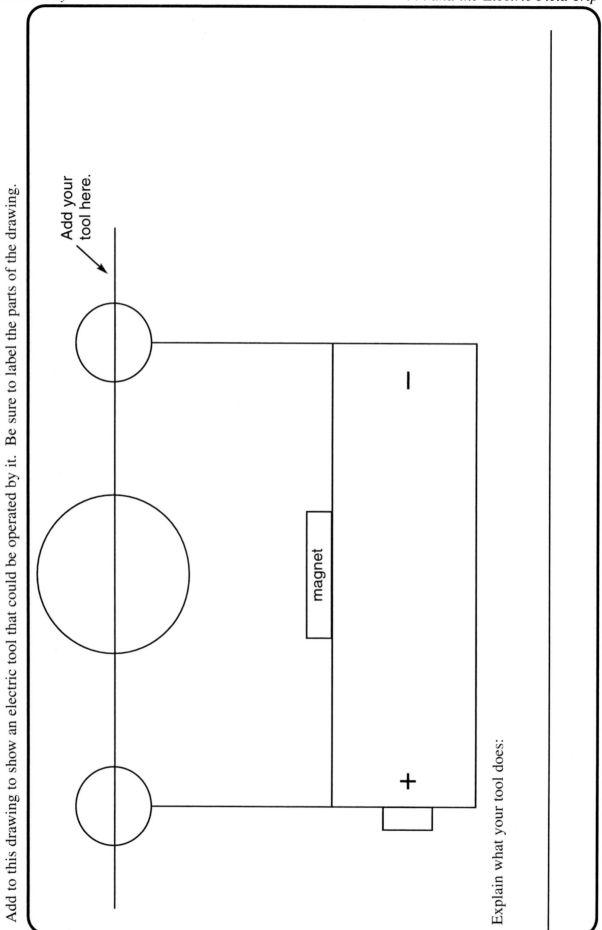

Add your tool here.

magnet

I

+

Explain what your tool does:

Our Power Plant Trip *(a play)*

The Story: Ms. Frizzle and her students make a fantastic journey through the power plant and back to their school (pages 18–43).

Activity: Students take a trip through the power plant, just as Ms. Frizzle's class did. (This will serve as one of the culminating activities for this unit.)

Materials

- transparencies of scenery (pages 38–43)
- script of Our Power Plant Trip (pages 44 and 45)

Preparation

- Enlarge the pictures on pages 38–43 and make transparencies of each scene. Then color them.
- Have students create title and end pictures. These may be done on a computer. Make transparencies of these title and end pictures to add at the beginning and end of the play.
- Hang a bedsheet from the ceiling to serve as a screen, or conduct this lesson in a room with a large wall surface on which the scenery can be projected.

Procedure

1. Explain that the students will be taking a trip through the power plant, just as Ms. Frizzle did with her students. The trip will begin in the power plant and end back at school.
2. Select students to read the script while the others walk across the projected image in groups of two or three. You may wish to rotate readers in order to include more students.
3. Project the transparencies onto the bedsheet or a large wall. If the bedsheet technique is used, the audience will sit on one side of the screen as the cast moves behind the screen with the images projected over them. If the wall is used, the audience will sit in front of the projector, facing the wall. The cast moves near the wall, passing through the image. A rotation of cast and audience can be arranged. After students have passed through the image, they take the seats of students in the audience who then assume the role of cast members.

audience on other side of bedsheet

bedsheet hung from ceiling

Closure

- Compare the scene inside the motor with the small motor made with a battery and magnet.
- Have students write an illustrated summary of the power plant trip.
- Invite other classes and parents to see the performance.

(1) The Furnace and (2) The Boiler

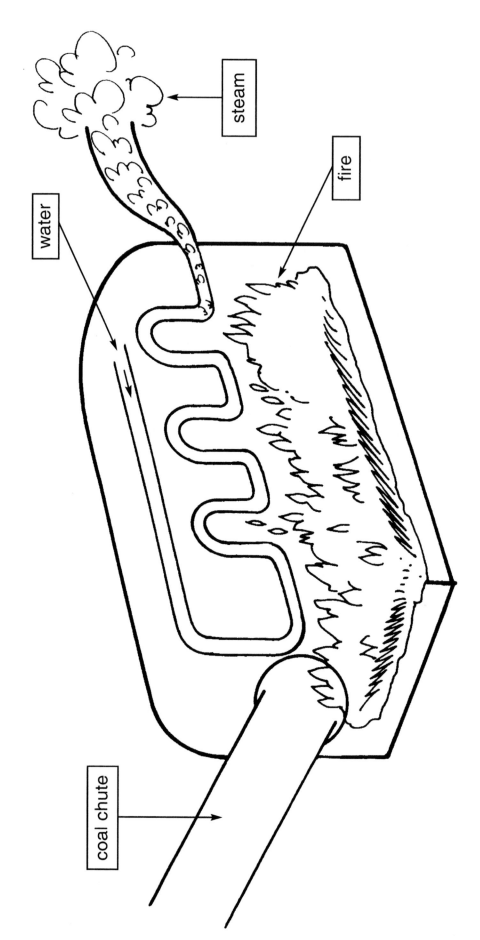

steam

fire

water

coal chute

(3) The Turbine

(4) The Generator

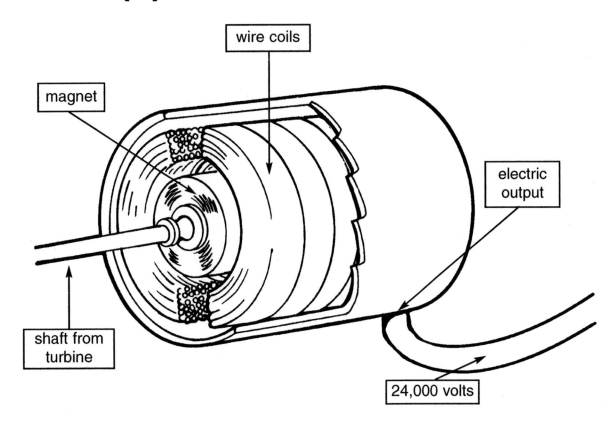

(5) The High–Voltage Wire

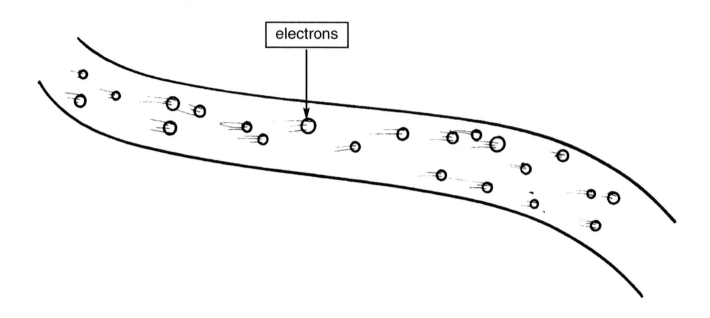

(6) Through the Transformers

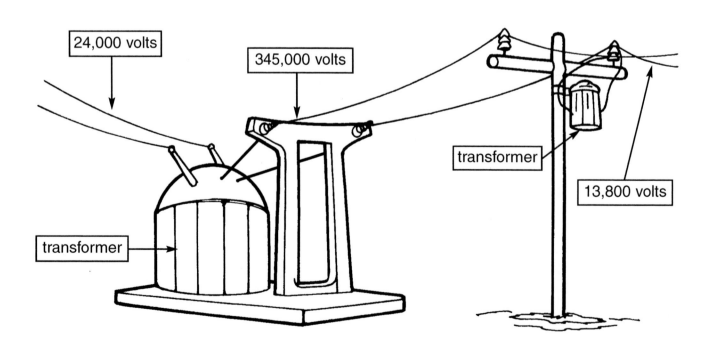

(7) Through a Light Bulb and Toaster

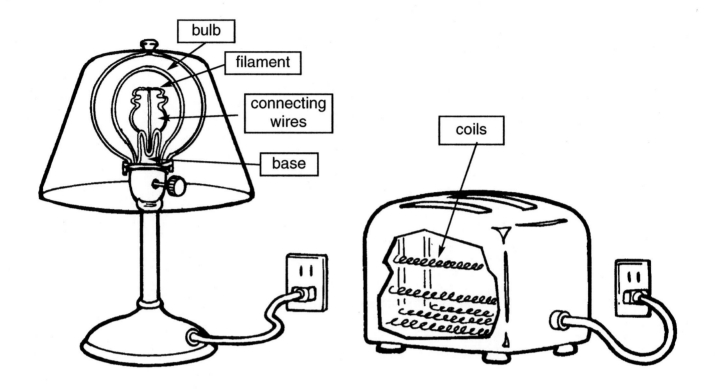

bulb

filament

connecting wires

base

coils

(8) Through the Motor

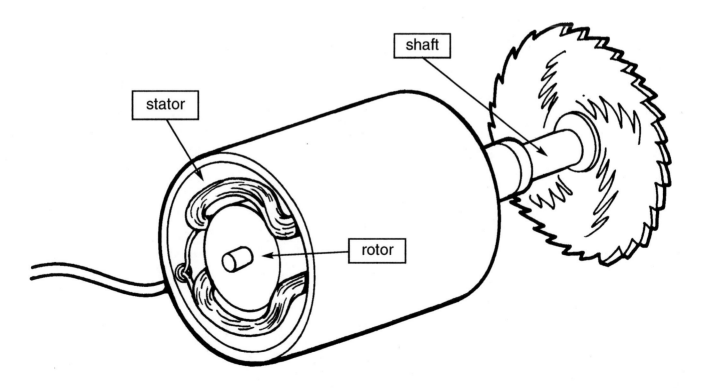

shaft

stator

rotor

(9) Inside the Motor

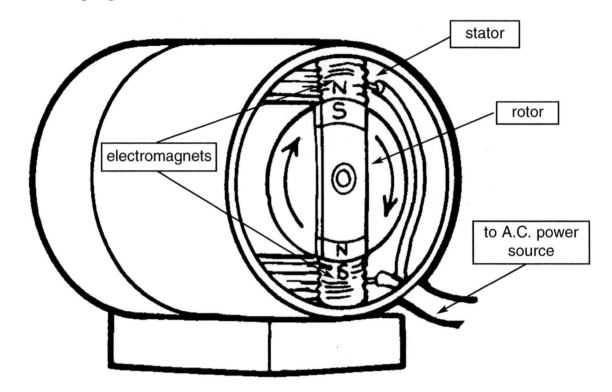

(10) Stuck in the Switch

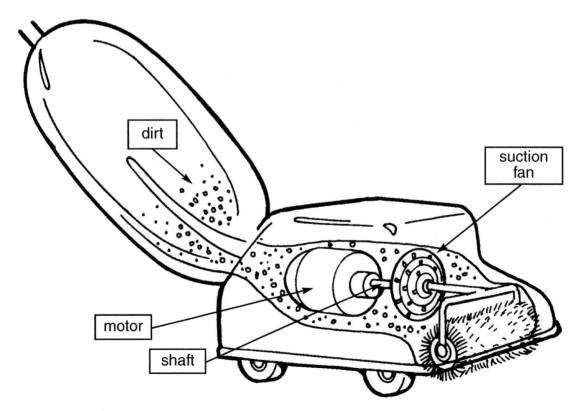

(11) On Our Way Again

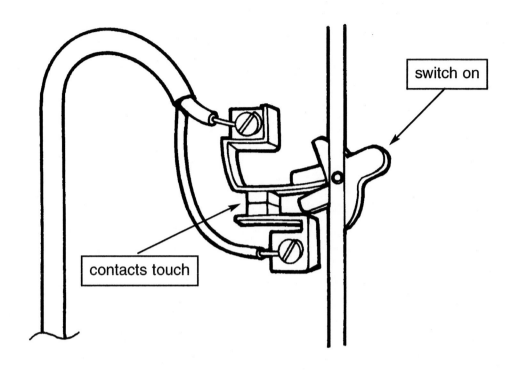

switch on

contacts touch

(12) Back at School at Last!

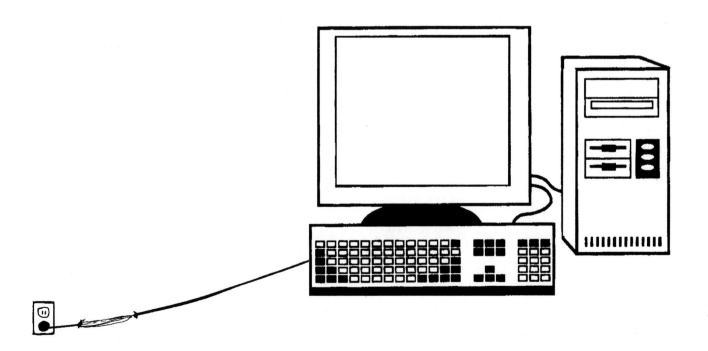

Our Power Plant Trip *(cont.)*

(Script)

As this script is read, two or three students should pass in front of the projected image. There are two scenes where no cast members should appear. These are marked *(no cast)*. You may wish to have a student other than the narrator use a pointer to indicate appropriate parts of these images.

Narrator: We are about to go on a *fantastic* field trip to learn how electricity reaches our businesses, homes, and schools. Get ready to travel with us as we begin in the . . .

Furnace: furnace at the power plant. We are dumped into the furnace with the coal. Here we are surrounded by flames burning up the coal. Don't worry, we are wearing insulated suits so we don't burn. We move into the . . .

Boiler: boiler overhead where we find pipes carrying water. The heat from the burning coal boils the water, changing it into steam. Hang onto each other! We are being pushed by the steam pressure through the pipe and into the . . .

Turbine: turbine. Oh no! Now we are going through whirling blades inside the turbine. The steam is turning the blades around and around and around. We are spinning out of the fan and onto the shaft. We are now sliding into the next part of the . . .

Generator: generator. Here is the place where electricity is made. The generator is HUGE! A magnet inside it is turned by the shaft, and the moving magnet makes the electric current which runs into the . . .

High Voltage Wire: high–voltage wire. Now we are shrinking to the size of electrons and flowing along with them through the wire. Electrons are jumping all around us, making the current. Wow! The voltage is 24,000 volts now. Let's follow the electrons through the lines toward the town. First we need to pass through . . .

Transformer: *Use pointer, no cast.* Here the voltage is increased to 345,000 volts so it has the transformer's power to travel longer distances. Steel transmission towers carry the wires to another transformer. This time the voltage is lowered to 13,800 volts so it can be used by factories and large businesses. Another transformer lowers the voltage to 110 and 220 volts so it can be used in our homes. Follow the electrons into a . . .

Light Bulb and Toaster: light bulb, where the filament heats up and glows as electric current passes through it. Inside the toaster, we follow the electric current through the coils, making them red hot so the bread is toasted. It's too hot to stay here, so we'll race on to . . .

Our Power Plant Trip *(cont.)*

(Script)

Motor: a motor which is driving a saw. The motor has a cylinder called a *rotor*, which is turning very fast. The rotor has a shaft attached to it, which is spinning. The spinning shaft is attached to the saw blade that is also spinning so it can cut the wood. Wow! All this is making us dizzy. Let's stop for a while and see what makes a motor work.

Inside a Motor: *Use pointer, no cast.*

1. An electromagnet is attached to the *stator* in the motor that doesn't move.

2. Another magnet is attached to the *rotor* which rotates.

3. The north pole of the stator magnet pulls on the south pole of the motor magnet. This makes the rotor turn.

4. The alternating current in the wire coil changes direction. This makes the poles of the stator magnet switch places.

5. Now the south pole of the electromagnet is next to the rotor magnet's south pole. These poles are the same, so they push each other away. This makes the rotor turn away from the electromagnet's south pole.

6. The current keeps alternating, so the rotor keeps turning.

Stuck in a Switch: Oh no! Our journey has come to a stop. We are stuck since someone switched off the power. There is a gap that the electrons can't flow across.

This gives us a chance to look at how a vacuum cleaner works. The shaft leading from the motor turns a fan and brush. The fan pulls in air, and the brush sweeps up dirt. The fan pulls the air and dirt into a bag.

On Our Way: Yes! Someone finally turned the switch on so we and the electrons can leap across and continue our travels back to . . .

School: school! We pass through the wall socket and jump out of a hole in the insulation of the wire leading into one of the computers in our classroom.

Narrator: It sure feels great to be back in our classroom. Our teacher will have the frayed wire fixed before it starts a fire or shocks someone.

We hope you enjoyed coming along on our field trip. Next time you flip a light switch or turn on a motor, think of the journey the electric current took to get there.

Post-Assessment

Activity: Students will again draw how power reaches the plug.

Materials

- copies of page 5, How Does the Power Reach the Plug?
- student copies of How Does the Power Reach the Plug? completed before the unit
- rulers
- pens or crayons

Procedure

Explain that the students will be completing another copy of the picture which shows how electricity reaches the plug in the wall (page 5). Tell them to first sketch their picture in pencil, including labels for the parts, and then trace over it with pen or crayons if they wish.

Closure

- After students complete the task, distribute their original drawings and let them compare. Discuss what they have learned in this unit.
- Keep both copies of the drawings to use as assessment of student progress.

════ How Do We Use Electricity? ════

Activity: Students will add to the list begun before the unit (page 4).

Materials

- chart made at the beginning of the unit
- lined chart paper
- colored pens
- construction paper
- magazines showing electrical devices
- scissors
- glue

Procedure

- Give each student a piece of paper and have each one write at least three things which use electricity but are not included on the list.
- Select items from the student's new list to add to the chart.

Closure

- Have students make a collage of magazine pictures showing items which use electricity.
- Let them make a picture of a future appliance they could use which runs on electricity. This picture should be added to their collage.

Unit Extender

Most power plants offer tours. If one is located near your school, arrange to take the students. An alternative would be to have a representative from the power plant visit the class and tell them about how electricity is made for their area.

The Electric Game

The Story: Ms. Frizzle's class had a board game which tested what they had learned about electricity (pages 46 and 47).

Activity: Students combine their knowledge of electricity, magnetism, and constructing an electric circuit to create an electric board game.

Materials

- tester used in What Conducts Electricity lesson (page 31).
- large sheet of colored tagboard
- six insulated wires of various lengths (insulation stripped from the ends)
- 12 brass paper brads
- file cards

Preparation (This should be done with student assistance.)

- Construct the game board as shown. Have questions written on the file cards hanging beside the brad heads. Write the instructions as shown above the brad heads.
- Connect wires to the prongs of the brads on the back of the board. Place a piece of tape over each of them to hold the wires firmly.

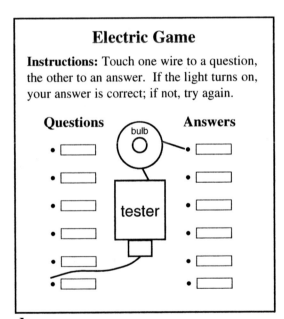

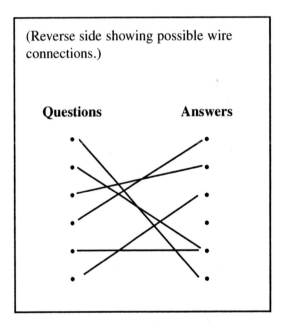

Procedure

1. Have students each write a question about magnets or electricity on one file card and the answer on another card. Tape these to the board next to the brads which are wired together.
2. Post the game board on the bulletin board. Place the tester in the center of the game board so that the wires will reach any of the connections.

Closure

Periodically place new cards on the board. Be sure to change the wire connections behind the board.

Answer Key

Compass at the Poles (page 19)

1. The standard horizontal compass would spin freely. A "dip compass" that moves vertically instead of horizontally would point straight down, north to north, or south to south.

2. Ten percent of Earth's magnetic field gradually shifts. Thus, navigational maps which show the deviations between the geographic North Pole and north magnetic pole become inaccurate after 100 years.

3. The "north" end of a magnet (e.g., compass needle) is really called the "north-seeking" end.

How Do Circuits Work? (page 30)

Parallel Circuit:

1. When one bulb is removed, the others continue to light. The current is not interrupted by the missing bulb since it can pass through the next wire and filament to continue on its path.

2. No

3. The electricity flows from the battery into each wire and through each filament and then back to the battery.

Seires Circuit:

4. When one bulb is unscrewed, the other bulbs go out.

5. None of the bulbs will light when one of them is loosened. The electricity must flow through the filament to reach the next wire.

6. The electricity flows from the battery into the first wire, through the first bulb's filament, and continues through the next wire and into bulb B, etc. It then flows back into the battery.

7. In a parallel circuit, when one bulb is burned out the others will still light. If one bulb burns out in a series circuit, no others can light.

8. The explanation for this is given in numbers 3 and 6 above.

Resources

Related Books

Burnie, David. *Eyewitness Science: Light*. Dorling Kindersley, Inc., 1992. This well-illustrated book has information regarding electricity, electromagnetic waves, and solar and light energy.

Macaulay, David. *The Way Things Work*. Houghton Mifflin Co., 1988. This book is filled with humorous cartoons which offer simple explanations for how things work, including electric motors, light bulbs, generators, batteries, and magnets.

Related Materials

Delta Education: P.O. Box 3000, Nashua, NH 03061-3000. (800) 442-5444 (*www.delta-ed.com*). This company supplies 2.5v bulbs, insulated wire, battery and bulb holders, magnets, and iron filings.

Edmund Scientific Co.: 191 East Gloucester Pike, Barrington, NJ 08007-1380. (800) 728-6999 or the on-line store at (*www.edsci.com/scientific*). This company supplies radiometers, solar batteries, and sunprint paper.

Radio Shack: This company supplies magnets, wire, and other electrical materials.